# Forest and Trees

## The Bible as a Whole

A new and different point of view

### H. Doyle Smith

**Aaron-Denburn Publishing**

H. Doyle Smith 1937-

Forest and Trees, The Bible as a Whole


ISBN  0-9647891-9-1          Paperbound
The Bible


©2005 H. Doyle Smith
All rights reserved


Aaron-Denburn Publishing
PO Box 9059
Canton, OH 44711
Hds12000@yahoo.com

# Contents

| | |
|---|---|
| Preface | iii |
| Introduction | 1 |
| In the Big Inning | 11 |
| The Characters | 17 |
| The Problem | 31 |
| Job, the Heart of the Bible | 37 |
| Human Attempts to Solve the Problem | 43 |
| The Gospels, God's solution to the problem | 47 |
| The Concluding Section | 57 |
| Summary | 61 |

# Preface

This is a book about the Bible. The Bible is a compilation of many chapters, each called "book," each written at a different time, under different circumstances, and by a different author with a different style. As a result the idea that they are separate and can be studied individually is a natural assumption.

But we say that the Bible was inspired by God. What does it indicate when we read that, "In the beginning God created the heavens and the earth," and we assume that God cannot inspire a complete and consistent narrative. The two ideas are mutually exclusive. Either God could inspire a complete and consistent book, or he is unable to create everything that is.

Over sixty years, I have learned that He did write a consistent narrative, and I have found five points that come from that knowledge. These points are

1. The Bible is a whole, with a consistent theme throughout.
2. The Bible is an introduction to God and His authority, and has no authority in and of itself
3. God is the creator, owner, and manager of the universe and under the ownership law of management is always right. The second law of management also applies, "When the Boss is wrong, refer to rule one.
4. We are only a small part of God's creation. We are limited by our environment, and cannot decide what is right and what is wrong except within that environment, and then only to the extent that the decision is approved by God.
5. You are an important part of God's creation, given a task, no matter how small, that God has felt important enough to have created you for. As such you will be provided with what you need.

As the son of a Southern Baptist preacher, I was involved with memory work, Sword Drill, and Adult Bible Reading for twenty-five years. The understanding that my family had was that the Bible was a collection of many books written by many different authors, all inspired by God. I accepted that idea (which is looking at the whole work as being separate pieces—Trees) but I was always thinking about the paradox of why God, who I understood to be omnipotent, as I still understand Him to be, could write a book that seemed to be so fragmented.

# Preface

It is easy to believe that the Bible is contradictory in places, and has different messages in others. The styles of the different books are different, since different people at different times wrote from different contexts. In an Old Testament literature class at Wake Forest University, I was exposed to the very human frailties of the different authors. I was shaken by the idea that each book could stand alone.

Over time, through meditation and thought, I came to ask myself if there was a coherent outline to the Bible. At some time I was introduced to the Shakespearian outline of seven parts: Introduction to the play, introduction to the characters, introduction to the problem (and the villain), statement of the problem, trial resolutions, final resolution, and conclusion. Since Shakespeare's outline developed at the same time as the translation of the Bible into English, I wondered if it might apply to the Bible as a whole, and found that it did. Wycliff, Tyndall, and the other translators must have had some idea of what books would fit, and how they would fit, in order to determine which books to translate. By having such an outline, they could look at the Bible as a whole (the forest.)

The principle inspiration for this book comes from the lives of my parents, both deceased, and so I would like to dedicate it to **Reverend Oscar Jackson Smith** and **Grace Francis Smith**, two dedicated and fervent Christians.

## Introduction

The Bible is a compilation of 66 books, poems, letters, and stories. It has philosophy, and other literary forms. At first glance it is fragmented, unorganized, contradicting itself, and subject to the irony that it has both authority and confusion. What does this idea indicate about the God who inspired it? With 1,600 years and numerous writers to plagiarize, He has failed to be able to write a coherent volume. This is a type of blasphemy, and a rather stupid concept. Why worship a God who can't even write a good book? How can anybody be, at the same time, all-knowing, all-powerful -- and incompetent? There must be some resolution to this quandary.

There is, but it's not very complimentary to mankind. The Bible has a clear, unmistakable, and coherent outline, a central theme that flows unchanged throughout, and all the elements of a great novel, but it requires a strong constitution to accept it and a clear mind to recognize it.

What makes a great novel? The best books all have certain things in common. First they have a central theme. Then they have a clear plot, a crisis, and a resolution. There must be a villain, a problem, and its solution. Moreover they must have a dynamic tension that allows the story to progress smoothly from one section to another. All the elements must be clearly stated, and there must be no loose ends that make us ask questions about what else happened. Despite all appearances, all these elements are present in the Bible. It is a coherent, well-written book.

It is easy to fail to see the forest for the trees. It is easy to fail to see the overall organization of any book if we dissect it and take each part separately. When we do this to the Bible we find that we have studied it, but not read it. Such study leads to some interesting concepts that take the place of the overall lessons of the Bible. Seventh Day Adventists accept the major lessons of the Bible, but add 21 more. They make an idol of the seventh day. That idol takes the place of, and supercedes the Biblical teaching that God is love—a love not dependent on which day of the week is holy.

We can make an idol of anything. We can say that it is "Wisdom" that is most important. We can say that the Bible gives us possession of a certain place. We can substitute anything for our conception of God and attempt to limit Him to what we understand. Even the Bible itself can be an idol. By limiting God to what the Bible says, we avoid having to make choices that are difficult. A certain "Christian" school chose to label Steinbeck's, Of Mice and Men, an unchristian book. This book deals with the love two men had for each other, and the choice of murder as a loving act on the part of one of them. That theme is foreign to the Bible, but is a real choice that some people have to make in certain circumstances.

# Introduction 3

The decision that the children should not have to face reality because it violated the school's idea of what is "right" is an illustration of the theme that permeates the Bible. Adam's sin was not choosing the "wrong" thing, but deciding for himself what was, in his own eyes, "wrong." The response God gave when He found Adam hiding was not, "Why are you naked?" but "Who told you that you were naked?" God didn't condemn Job for his unfaithfulness, but for his attempt to limit God to his understanding. And, in Acts, Peter was clearly told, "What I have called clean, don't you call unclean."

People like to dissect the Bible. They like to look at every part of the Bible as having the same impact as the whole Bible taken together. This attitude leads to some really silly circumstances. For example, a preacher made a sermon against the "Top Knot" hairdo because the Bible said, "Top Knot come down." When challenged, he recited the whole verse, "Let him who is on the housetop not come down." This verse enabled him to give his personal opinion of a hairstyle the force of divine disapproval. Dissecting the Bible makes an individual feel that he understands God and can speak for him.

The idea that God can be something that we do not understand is uncomfortable, but an essential concept if we are to work *with* God instead of at cross-purposes to Him. We try to become comfortable by making him fit into our comprehension. The essence of the Bible, however, is that

God will be whatever He wants, and we need to become comfortable with the understanding that God is, and will be, whatever He chooses.

The consequences of trying to restrict God to what we can understand are sometimes ludicrous. A certain minister proclaimed that God would punish Disney World by sending a hurricane because of a matter that related to homosexuality. When the hurricane did come that year the area devastated was the area around the minister's home base. Now this isn't a condemnation of this minister, but an illustration of how we can get into trouble by saying we know what God wants. The problem is simple. Is the minister wrong because he said God would punish with a hurricane, or is the minister being punished by God? God, like the 900-pound gorilla, sleeps wherever he chooses, not where man would place him.

When Moses asked God for his name, He replied, "I am whatever I am." That seemed be an answer to the question that was asked. People started assigning the name to God, and calling Him "I am." Another time Christ didn't answer the question asked and replied, "Render unto Caesar the things that are Caesar's and unto God the things that are God's." In both cases, the question was the man's and the reply was God's. People, feeling in control of the situation, assumed that the question controlled the answer, and limited the answer in one case to a name and in the other to taxes. In each case, God went far beyond the question, and gave an answer that revealed far more depth than man had expected.

# Introduction 5

God is whatever He is. The fact that man has tried to limit God to what he can understand has made man arrogant, and from other points of view, very stupid. Man says, "God is Love," and cannot understand why God would cause bad things to happen to good people. It is as if God had to live by man's understanding of Him. I have a wife whom I dearly love, but I would no more try to tell her about menstrual periods than walk to the moon. The subject is beyond my experience. If I chose to advise my wife on that subject, I would look almost as stupid as a minister trying to define and limit God.

Yet man, who cannot fully understand the realities of anything outside the experiences that God has given him, will tell God that he shouldn't take the life of a little child, because "God is Love." God is whatever He is, not what we can understand He is. The Jewish story of Abraham's (then called Abram) practical joke in Ur illustrates the stupidity of worshipping a God that can be understood.

Terah, Abram's father, was an idol maker in Ur, and made his living by making idols for the people to worship. Abram went into the shop during lunch one day, took an axe, and broke up all the idols but one. He put the axe in that idol's hand. When his father came back, he asked Abram who had destroyed the idols, and Abram told him that the idol with the axe had done it. Terah raged at him, saying, "You know that that idol can't do anything." Abram replied, "If the idol can't do anything, why do we worship it?" This question was enough to get the family expelled from Ur. People were comfortable with their worship of idols, and this question made them uncomfortable.

Groucho Marx once said that he wouldn't belong to a club that would allow him to belong. We are in the same boat as Groucho, when we worship a god that we can understand. If God is limited to what is within our understanding, He could not deal with the things that we have never experienced, and He would be of no use to us.

## The Nature of the Outline

The Bible is written in seven sections that each have a definite purpose. They are: an introduction to the story, an introduction to the characters, an introduction to the problem (and the villain), a statement of the problem (the crisis), possible human solutions to the problem, a resolution, and a conclusion wrapping up loose ends.

The introduction to the story takes one book, Genesis. Within Genesis, we have a definition of the assumptions that carry through the Bible. Those assumptions are followed by a description of man's attempts

# Introduction

to decide right from wrong and the consequences of those attempts. The last part is an illustration of how three different men:--a pragmatist, Abraham; a charlatan, Jacob; and a dedicated man, Joseph--each met the challenge of accomplishing what God wanted done.

The introduction to the characters, Exodus through Second Kings, tells us how we, as human beings, react to the real world and its challenges. Although there are some places that label things as sins, actions and their consequences are told forthrightly, and the nature of each action is clearly shown. This section starts by defining certain laws which are self-enforcing, and others that are purely meant to allow certain people to feel better than their neighbors. The latter are refuted in Romans and Hebrews, but for the sake of the story they are allowed to be given full force in this and several succeeding sections. The people, without any central authority established to allow coordination with each other, did some very strange things. To solve this lack of authority they asked for, and received a king. They established a kingdom that lasted until the exile.

The third section, introduction to the villain, starts by restating the history just completed, but judging and evaluating every action by the human understanding of, "God's Will." This brings about some interesting interpretations. David was supposed to be doing what they called, "God's Will," so Bathsheba couldn't exist. Her story did not square with their understanding. Kings who did no other good for their people than following the letter of the law were labeled "good," solely because they upheld the tyranny of the scriptures. The result of this tyranny was to create societies that separated themselves from their neighbors, even to the extent of divorcing their wives (divorce would later be condemned by Christ), making people worry about their sins, and create an abusive society. Eventually, in the book of Esther, the people ignore God completely.

There is only one chapter in the next section. Job deals with the problem addressed in the Bible. No matter how "righteous" Job was, God did with him whatever he willed. When Job and his friends tried to define God, God became so angry that he belabored Job with four chapters of a diatribe in response to his even attempting this impossible task. The book of Job spells out the nature of the theme of the Bible. A real understanding of the nature of Job helps us understand what the Bible is really about.

The next section tries to use human resources to resolve the problem of man's relationship to God. Psalms is meditation and soothing words. Proverbs tries to use witty sayings that mean different things to different people. Ecclesiastes is the work of a cynic. Song of Solomon says sex is capable of diverting us. Isaiah is a Polyanna. Jeremiah uses anger. Lamentations exhibits sadness. Ezekiel uses mysticism to convey that we are individually responsible. Daniel retreats into mysticism.

# Introduction

There are twelve other short attempts to solve the problem of how we relate to God, treating the problem in human terms.

Then the resolution follows. The four chapters of the Gospels tell us how God wants us to relate to him. Matthew looks to the traditions, and forms a bridge between what has passed before and this section. Mark describes what went on. Luke helps us to look forward, and John explains the principles that underlie the resolution.

Matthew also is the pragmatist, with specific statements about how we can satisfy God. Mark describes the actions that occurred during Jesus' life. Luke allows us to understand that we ourselves are involved in an ongoing cosmic relationship. John's theoretical understanding of the concepts involved shows that the ideas are realistic.

The last section wraps up the loose ends and shows that the story continues to be relevant. Romans and Hebrews make it clear that the laws of worship laid down in Leviticus no longer apply. True worship of God demands that cooperation with Him be important, and shows that ceremonies are only valuable for man's need, not God's. The illustrations of how a person might work with God in practical matters help us to realize how we can cooperate with God if we want to.

This section concludes with an illustration of what might be a blessed hereafter. The dream in the Revelation of John is clearly a dream, but the atmosphere of a great, grand, and pleasant future, no matter how illogical, spells out that the kingdom of God will prevail.

## In the Big Inning

A little boy informed his father that God had invented baseball. When asked why he thought that, the little boy replied, "Well, there it is, 'In the big inning, God created...'"

The first chapter of Genesis, and a part of the second, deals with a critical assumption. God created order out of chaos. In laymen's terms, order exists in the world. This is a critical difference between Christianity and existentialism. To accept the Bible, we have to accept that the seeming irrational twists and turns that we see are not aberrations, but have a logical place in the scheme of things.

A scientist who is also a Christian, studies order, and tries to understand that order. When scientists push their ideas as if science controlled God, instead of God controlling science, they are ignoring this assumption. Miracles are not the subject of scientific study. To prove a scientific explanation for a miracle is a statement that God can't ignore science. The scientist who does this is setting up science as an idol, attempting to limit God, and placing himself and his point of view in a difficult position.

The theory of the "big bang" is just that, a theory. A little boy skipping rocks observes that the waves get wider apart as they get further from the place that the stone hit. He observes that waves created by a boat consist of three waves that get wider and lower as the boat goes away. He observes that thunder at a distance has a lower pitch than thunder close at hand. Then he hears the scientist ignore this observation (that waves lengthen over distance) and state that the Doppler Effect is the only way that the red shift can occur. Having observed that waves lengthen over distance, and that the red shift involves waves lengthening over distance, he repudiates the scientist's theory, and tries to find a substitute. Creationism isn't biblical, but a result of the arrogance of scientists.

The nature of this first part of Genesis is to determine that there is order in the world. The attempt to use it as a substitute for scientific thinking is repudiated by the Bible itself; God did not create the sun or moon until the fourth "day." He called the light "day," so day to Him did not mean twenty-four hours, but light, and light could mean any number of days, or years.

In this part also is the purpose of man. It is to be noted that God told him to, "be fruitful, multiply, replenish the earth, and subdue it." These instructions give us a purpose in life. They are also very practical. However, when Onan spilled his seed upon the ground, the writer called his action a "sin" because it violated this instruction. Calling anything a sin violates the principal theme of the Bible by judging the action of someone as if the author was God himself, but the Bible is about human behavior and humans act that way.

# The Human Need for Cooperation

The second part of Genesis spells out that human trait of calling things sinful and judging the action of someone as if the observer was God himself. It also spells out the consequences of acting this way. Using Adam and Eve as examples, it shows that mankind does decide for itself what is "right" and what is "wrong." This all too human trait is stronger in women, and the allocation of its origin to Eve is a very astute observation. It is impractical to explain every act to a child as if he could thoroughly understand all the ramifications. For the species to survive, it is necessary to tell the child that running out into traffic is "wrong," as is sticking a paper clip into an electrical outlet. There are many things we shouldn't do, and in most cases if we want to get on with our lives, it is easier to call it "wrong" and not do them. The problem arises when (to paraphrase) "Everyone does what is 'right' in his own eyes." The consequences of this attitude are illustrated in the section from Cain and Abel to Noah. Cain killed Abel, and anarchy became the order of the day. God tried to eliminate the problem by eliminating all the people except Noah and his family. Then Noah's sons called Ham's laughing at his father a "sin" and it started all over again.

We cannot survive as a species if we are constantly at odds with each other. Cooperation, or coordination, is necessary for our survival, and each person deciding what is "right" or "wrong" destroys the chance of that cooperation.

## The Patriarchs

The third section of Genesis deals with four examples of how God can relate to man. The first example is Abraham (Abram) and illustrates the pragmatist. The Jewish apocryphal tale mentioned above could easily explain why Abram felt that he had to be careful what other people thought of him, and could explain why he was so careful not to offend.

## Abraham

Usually when Abraham met some crisis in his life he found a peaceful way to resolve it. His faith that idols didn't control his life, and his belief that there was a God and order in the world, allowed him to live peaceably with his neighbors. Unfortunately, his neighbors included the worshippers of the Baals, among whom was the God Moloch. These neighbors had the idea that Moloch could only be satisfied by the sacrifice of the eldest son.

Later Rome would fight three wars with these Moloch worshippers in Carthage, but Abraham had no such power when the neighbors demanded the sacrifice of Isaac. Since Abraham understood that God would not be placated by such a sacrifice and that the idol Moloch had no power, his faith enabled him to circumvent the requirement by substituting a ram. This faith that God was greater than any idol became the basis of his worship.

Abraham is a very human individual. That he established the idea that God was greater than what people can understand is a major step in establishing our religion.

## Isaac

Isaac is a son's typical response to a strong father. He served as a foil to his father, and later to his also strong son, but he was not a strong person himself. Not able to understand and assert himself, he tried to avoid problems rather than face them. Given that he had a beautiful wife, when he ran into a situation when there might be a confrontation because of her, he called her his sister. When his wells were contested he let the other party have them. Such a person leaves a vacuum in life that is usually filled by a son. For Isaac, that son was Jacob.

## Jacob

We like to believe that God wants moral followers. If that were the case, Jacob would never have been mentioned. He and his mother connived to steal the birthright and blessing from his brother. He and his mother lorded it over the neighbors and looked down on them. Yet God gave him His blessing. It is human for a person to think of himself as more important than other people around him. A dream came to Jacob that corroborated this, and subsequent events seemed to bear it out in his mind. Even though we think of Jacob as a scoundrel, it is clear that the Lord did not reject him because of that.

## Joseph

The story of Joseph, no matter how boring, brings a new approach to the idea of how we should act. His ideal willingness to live with whatever God placed in his path gives us an example of obedience to God under stressful circumstances. The circumstances were not the circumstances of the wealthy, and his story changes as his circumstances change. But Joseph is not the everyday individual. God calls some people to specific tasks, but Josephs, Joan of Arcs, and Jesuses are rare. That Abraham, Isaac, and Jacob are ordinary people is clear, and the use of the phrase, "The God of Abraham, Isaac, and Jacob", omitting Joseph, shows that people are accepted by God, even though only a few are chosen to a specific task.

The end of the book of Genesis states the purpose of the Bible. Joseph said, "The evil you planned to do me has by God's design been turned to good." We are not to label what God chooses "wrong."

# The Characters

The second section of the Bible is an introduction to the characters that play a part in this story. There are three parts to this section of the Bible. The first is the story of how a somewhat amorphous group (the Hebrews) is separated out and given an identity. Overlaying this is the common set of rules and rituals that identify this group as separate from all others. The third part gives the history of this people, from the anarchic conditions that existed when no regular form of coordination was available, through the development of a monarchy to the decline and eventual extinction of their state.

The characters that are part of the Bible story are not necessarily individuals. The principle characters are God and the Hebrew nation.

## God

God is defined in a few short words—whatever He is He is. We are made in the image of God, and so whatever we are we are as well. These two understandings are the elements of a peaceful existence on earth.

A certain individual was invited to lunch. He found that there was a gallon of wine that the host expected to last for several weeks. The drunk drank the gallon at one sitting, all the time saying, "I'm not an alcoholic." Failure to accept himself as an alcoholic ended his ability to function well in society, and made him a lonely individual.

His host told the story of his experience in an army mess hall. The mess sergeant decided to ride him unmercifully one day. If he used hot water, the mess sergeant said he should use cold. If he used cold, the mess sergeant said he should use hot. After eight hours of such abuse, the host moved his hand toward a convenient knife and made a move to stab the mess sergeant. The chief cook announced that the shift was over before anything occurred, but the host acknowledged that he was a murderer. Only the timely intervention of the chief cook had saved the lives of both the host and the mess sergeant.

The guest would not acknowledge that the host was a murderer, but the acknowledgement had allowed the host to know what circumstances would cause him to commit murder, and enabled him to look for and avoid them. He had accepted himself as he was, and did not try to be what he was not.

Accepting ourselves as we are is a key to contentment. Attempting to be what we are not is an exercise in frustration.

God must be allowed to be whatever He is also. In Bosnia, where God is said to be a Roman Catholic by one group, and their neighbors say He is Orthodox or Allah, we create the results of men's action in deciding for God what He is. Those results end in war and destruction. An attempt to limit God to what we understand is the surest way possible to make our lives unlivable.

## The Hebrew Nation

The rise and fall of the Hebrew Nation is the heart of this section of the Bible, but a nation is made up of people, and it is best described through the actions of those people, so we find that this section contains some of the most memorable stories of individual characters.

We have already met some characters, but those characters have only a role to play as a reference and a common ancestral bond. From Exodus to Joshua we learn about how a group can achieve a common identity, and the principle ritual that the Hebrews developed to maintain that identity. And we start to develop the characters that actively participate in the story with Moses. The patriarchs gave us an example of a pragmatist, an appeaser, a con-man, and a person dedicated to a specific task. Now we are to meet some people who have a role in History.

## Identifying Who We Are Talking About

This section of the Bible starts off with the identification of the Hebrews as a separate people. No story can be easy to follow if the people in it are not identifiable and identified. It's true that the characters told about in this section are similar to ones we know, but we understand any story better if we can name the characters.

Essentially this part of the Bible is the story of the actions of Moses and Joshua. Like Joseph, Moses was a dedicated man, not superhuman, or bigger than life, but dedicated. Also like Joseph, Moses didn't push himself into the position he held, but acted only as God directed. Joshua followed Moses as the leader of the people, and summarized the requirement that the Hebrews were identified as worshippers of one God.

As at the beginning, some principles are laid out in this section too. The laws of the Pentateuch are a discussion of some principles and rules that are either self-enforcing, or ritual. The ritual laws are dealt with later in the epistle of Romans and Hebrews. They help set the people apart and identify them as different, but are not essential to either survival or enjoyment. The self-enforcing laws are common sense rules that have consequences if they are broken. They do not require the authority or backing of God to be necessary, but enforce themselves by the consequences if they are ignored. Principle among these are those that are collected in the Ten Commandments.

## The Ten Commandments Are Not Religious

Looking at the Ten Commandments as if they were not a part of the Bible is interesting. When we do, we find that they are a self-enforcing set of rules that apply anywhere. To call them a part of any religion is to limit them, and by limiting them we create a less than perfect life for ourselves.

"You will have no other gods before me" is the first commandment. God gives us the purpose of doing together what we cannot do separately. We have the responsibility to cooperate with each other. We are a community. Each of us is responsible to the other for order and cooperative effort. No other authority than God can allow us to cooperate when there are so many different needs, interests, and responsibilities.

The problems in Bosnia did not come from the wishes of the people to worship God. They came from the worship of the "god" of the Roman Catholic, the "god" of the orthodox, and the "Allah" of the Muslims. Each had limited his "god" to what he understood, and set that "god" up as an idol. Some choose to designate the Bible as god, and say that, whatever the Holy Spirit says, the Bible is the infallible word of God.

In such a case, the Bible becomes no more than an idol. Whenever this first commandment is ignored, man's attempts become confrontational, and humanity suffers.

In line with this understanding, the second commandment, "You will not make statues and idols to worship" goes further. Statues and images are firm appearances in a transient world. Many homes have pictures on the wall of the children who grew up in that home. The parents like to remember them as they used to be. When the children visit, even if they are fifty years old, the parents think of them as children, and treat them as such. In such a way they are acting inappropriately for the current situation. There are two other ways this rule enforces itself. When the Jews had been dispersed, they chose to return to what was their life was before, rather than face the challenges of a different situation. By holding on to scriptures that applied to a different era, they became stultified, and unable to adapt to conditions as they were in a different time. A major part of the problems defined in the third section of the Bible arise from this attempt to enforce an inappropriate set of rules and regulations. To make images is to hold on to the past after the conditions of the past are no longer appropriate.

The next commandment, "You shall not bow down to (images) or serve them," is probably the hardest task that any human can recognize and avoid. A man who would vote for a yellow dog if he were a (Democrat, Republican) is not able to look at the interest of the whole country except through the eyes of the party. Such people allow the country to slip into an "us versus them" attitude. A Baptist who says that all Roman Catholics are going to hell is similarly making an image of the church. Christ determines who will go to heaven. His comment that "Not everyone who says 'Lord, Lord' will enter the kingdom of heaven" makes this point.

Such is the case when we try to limit God to the Bible by saying, "The Bible is infallible." The Bible then becomes an image, rather than an introduction to God.

The next Commandment has often been linked to vulgarity, but vulgarity is not necessarily any part of taking the Lord's name in vain. Taking the Lord's name in vain can be compared to the preacher mentioned above who said God would send a hurricane to another and received the hurricane himself instead. God does not give the power to speak for Him to any person, even the Pope.

The next commandment is more directed to the individual's best interest. A man worked in the naval shipyards during World War II. He was dedicated to his task and did not take Sundays, or any day, off to rest. After a period of several months, he developed health problems and became an invalid. We are not able to work continuously without rest. Moreover, we have a circadian rhythm in our physical makeup. If we choose to ignore the need for rest, we become disoriented and subject to disease. The meaning of this commandment is that we should do what is necessary for our health. The Sabbath can be any day that we chose or that is required of us, but we must rest.

Fathers and mothers have a particularly important role in developing children as members of the community so that they will be competent individuals. The Bible supports those efforts. Children will be expected to obey their parents, so that they may live effective lives in the community in which they live. A child should honor his father and mother. The mother and father should be worthy of that honor.

Violence always destroys whatever it is directed against. The commandment "You shall not kill" is directed toward this. Violence of any type kills something in a person. It also diminishes trust and safety. Violence against any person cannot be tolerated or excused. Violence includes murder, but is not limited to it. Later we will find the "Golden Rule" to read, "Do unto others as you would have them do unto you." There is a corollary to this, restated as, "What you have done unto others, you want done unto you." If you kill someone, you have set the example, and that example followed to its end would mean that all people are dead, so don't set the example. Do not kill.

Adultery is the betrayal of one person by another when he has committed himself not to do so. Failure to live up to such commitments creates disharmony, whether in marriage or elsewhere. Contracts are such commitments, though not in the marriage context. Nothing can be accomplished in life if we are unable to rely on the word of those with whom we work, so do not commit adultery in any context. You should not betray your neighbor.

The consequences of such betrayal are tragic. Ellen DeGeneres gave a great deal of publicity to her private affairs. They were no one's business but her own and Anne Heche's. The affair could not survive such betrayal. Not only was this a betrayal of what should have been private, but it encouraged the belief that such things are public knowledge, and that everyone should know about them.

Betrayal in marriage includes betrayal with another, but that other does not need to be a person. Workaholics often choose their job as more important than their mate. Adultery, betrayal, creates far more problems than any other error. A person should never betray another's trust in him.

Theft destroys a person's ability to complete what has been started. Sufficient theft will make all activities impossible. Theft is not limited to things, however. We can steal a person's reputation by gossip.

To provide security for every person requires that what is said agrees with what is actually true. Failure to provide truthful statements makes it impossible to believe what is said. A citizen will not give false evidence against his neighbor, anyone else, or for any cause whatsoever. A person should speak the truth.

There are sufficient things available and sufficient means by which those things that are needed can be obtained. A citizen will not set his heart on his neighbor's house, car, spouse, etc or any of his neighbor's possessions. A person should respect the property of others. If something of your neighbor's interests you, duplicate it.

## Other "Laws"

Almost all of the "laws" set out in this part of the Bible are either ritual or self-enforcing. In Exodus 22:21-23, we find that God has now brought war to Israel because of that country's treatment of the Palestinians. God did not have to do that. The consequences of the Israelis' actions are human reactions to such abuse. So it is with many of "God's Laws." Ignoring them is not a sin against God, but a reduction in our ability to live life to the fullest.

Laws of the other type, ritual laws, are made for man's benefit. By the celebration of the Seder, Jews choose to remember something that is common to all of them. When they meet they have a common reference point and context that allows them to communicate with each other. In the days of the Baals, their common beliefs allowed them to avoid the requirements of human sacrifice that the community would have placed on them by substituting animal sacrifice. This mutual support enabled them to support each other and maintain their beliefs.

## **The Basic Story**

(Since the Bible itself is the best source of the history of the Hebrews, there is no need to repeat it here.) The underlying story begins with Moses' life, and his action in separating the Hebrews from their life in Egypt, carrying them through the wilderness, and their establishment as a people in Palestine. The ending of this part has Joshua stating, "Choose you this day whom you will serve, but as for me and my house we will serve the Lord." After this time, the Hebrews were established residents in Palestine. There is a break in the story here before the next part begins. Up to this time we have been as interested in laws as in the story. Now we will deal with people.

Even though the Hebrews were established, they were not a nation as such. The book of Judges shows the effect of having no central authority that people can turn to that is accepted by all the people. When passions were aroused, they killed all the Benjaminites, and then said they were sorry. We do the same thing now. These very human people finally came to realize that they needed ordinary everyday guidance, so that there could be a resort to it, instead of their own opinions, when there was a disagreement. They asked Samuel, who everyone respected, to give them one.

Samuel was a human being, and all human beings are imperfect. The effect of seeing Samuel as a perfect example has led many people to overlook his jealousy, and bias, as well as other inferences that can be made from his actions. Moreover, since his party has had the advantage of victory, and victors are the ones who write history, we have to look at what is said about him with care.

Saul was a handsome man, taller than all the others, but he had no example of what was required of a king to follow. Samuel anointed him as king, then had him publicly selected by lot. Saul was shy, and hid from the people at the time the lots were cast. The people saw this and some questioned his ability to be king. He was a good warrior, however, and led the people in battle with some success.

The problem with Saul was that he had no example or training to teach him how to be a king. Knowing his own weaknesses, he began to fear challenges, and did not understand what it took to inspire cooperation. Any man placed in his position without any training would make mistakes, and Saul was no exception. Small things caused friction, and Saul lost Samuel's support when Saul decided that Samuel wasn't needed when there was a job that only Samuel could do.

God's purpose in choosing Saul was not to make Saul king forever, but to have him serve as a foil to teach David what he needed to be king. David, having been raised from the people and trained to be king, became an example of what a king should be. God gave him the kingdom, but refused to allow him to build a religious temple. Since the purpose of the civil government, as we will later find out, is to demand little of the people and extract that little unmercifully, and the purpose of religion is to demand perfection, with the sure understanding that people will fail to succeed in that, David's kingship is considered ideal.

His son Solomon had not been raised from the people. Having had power in his hands all his life, he did not understand that people have to be able to live in order to effectively accomplish anything. He spent the country's wealth on a grandiose temple so that at his death, those who weren't able to live their own lives because of his demands rebelled and separated the country into two countries. These two countries were not able to protect themselves from foreign invaders and eventually disappeared.

This section of the Bible has shown us the historical example of what has happened in the past to real people; the problem arises when we look at it as an example of how we should act in the future.

# The Problem

The role of the next five books of the Bible, I and II Chronicles, Ezra, Nehemiah and Ester, can be determined in three ways. First a comparison of the subjects of these books with the theme of all the rest of the books of the Bible shows that they are in direct opposition to the theme that permeates them. Second, a comparison of their teaching and the Gospel's teaching shows that Christ condemned or refuted everything that these books taught. Third, an application of common sense shows that these books propose nonsensical solutions.

## Comparison with the Theme

When Adam decided that he should be embarrassed because he was naked, God asked him, "Who told you that you were naked. Have you eaten of it (the tree of the knowledge of good and evil)?" If he had eaten from that tree (if he had decided for himself that nakedness was 'bad') he could have become embarrassed. If someone else had told him that nakedness was bad he could have been embarrassed. In no other way would he have taken any other notice of his nakedness. Adam had decided for himself that nakedness was evil.

Joseph stated at the end of Genesis, "Is it for me to put myself in God's place? The evil you planned to do me has, by God's design, been turned to good." The characters in the second section accepted that there were consequences, and were not embarrassed by their "sins." Instead, they went about their lives without looking back.

Job states the theme best. "I know that you are all powerful: what you conceive you can perform. I was the man who misrepresented your intentions with my ignorant words. You have told me about great works that I cannot understand, about marvels which are beyond me, of which I know nothing."

The prophet's very human attempts to come to terms with this reality show that they understood that their relationship with God was difficult from their point of view because God was beyond their control. In the New Testament when Peter tells God that he has been clean, God replies "What I have called clean don't you call unclean."

The theme of the Bible (that God is all powerful and we are not to decide for Him what is "right" or "wrong," "good" or "evil") is clearly stated.

## The Gospels and Ezra/Nehemiah

Christ made it clear that divorce was never something God intended to be. "... What God has united, human beings must not divide ... Now I say this to you: 'anyone who divorces his wife ... is guilty of adultery.'" This unequivocal statement is in direct opposition to Ezra's demand that the people divorce certain of their wives to maintain "purity."

# The Problem 33

Jesus responds to this so called "purity" by saying, "Don't you understand that nothing that goes into one from outside can make that person 'unclean?' . . .It is what comes out of someone that makes a person 'unclean.'"

The return of the Israelites to Jerusalem, in order to worship, is similarly commented on. "You will not worship in Jerusalem or on this mountain, but in spirit and in truth." God told Abraham that he would be a blessing to all nations, and he has been. Many understandings that we have, have come from the life of Abraham and his descendents, but this blessing has been one of responsibility, not privilege. The idea that we need to go to any one place to worship God is ludicrous. The belief that there is something spiritual about any particular place makes that place an idol and attempts to limit God.

Ezra dwelt on the need to atone for sin. Christ said, "All sins will be forgiven, except refusing to work with the Holy Spirit." There are six billion people in the world. There are more insects and animals than people. God not only created them, but He created the place that they live in. How, then, can you expect God to waste his time on any sin that you can do? Moreover, what's done is done and cannot be undone. What's important is what you will do next, not what you have done "wrong." The time spent on worrying about sin causes the worrier to make sin his idol instead of worshipping God.

Almost every teaching or example that Ezra develops is condemned or refuted by Christ.

## **Common Sense**

God is omniscient. That means that He is able to see what's going on everywhere. No man can claim to know what is going on outside his experience. Yet we have preachers who tell us what God wants of us as if each of them were able to know things that are beyond the possibility of his knowledge. Usually this "knowledge" is based on some "authority," and usually that authority is some book or concept that is supposed to encompass the universe. All books, including the Bible, are limited to what the author wants told. The process of writing a book passes through many screens that dilute the ability of the book to be authoritative. The author has only what's in his sight to write about. That sight has to be condensed to fit in the form of the book. He uses his own understanding of language to express the thought. The reader uses his understanding of the language and has to fit the thought into his experience. Each of these screens diminishes the ability of the reader to understand the reality that underlies the written word. That reality is far greater than the words of the author. Why then is the Bible so important?

***The Bible is our introduction to God!!!***

## The Nature of the Problem Section

The Chronicles start with a revision of the history of the kingdom of Israel. But the difference is subtle. Since the purpose of the Chronicles is to establish a ritual and give it authority, the career of David can have no personal faults. Bathsheba does not exist for the Chronicler. What is not grand in the story of David is assigned to Satan. Form and order are emphasized. Then the lessons begin. Each king is mentioned in turn. If there are no events to record, the mention of the king involved shows only one thing, his loyalty to the ideal that the Chronicler has set for him. For Rehoboam, "he did wrong in not setting his heart on seeking Yahweh." For Jehoshaphat, "He was the grandson of Jehosaphat who sought the Lord with all his Heart. Joash did what Yahweh regards as right." Each king is judged only on whether he agreed with what the priests considered "right."

The result of this limitation of God's will to what the priests thought was "right" is found in Ezra/Nehemiah. These books are confused chronologically, but still show that the rigid straightjacket of the ritualists created a situation where people were judged by how faithfully they followed the ritual, not by what they contributed to the community.

The progression of the problem of people deciding what was "right" and what was "wrong" proceeds to the book of Esther, which dispenses with God altogether.

This section demonstrates that "right" and "wrong" are not the best way to judge what anyone does.

## Job, the Heart of the Bible

The theme of the Bible is expounded most clearly in Job. Given that the story is of a man who is "good," and who is first deprived of everything, and then restored to everything, we look at the story as a feel-good parable. Strip the saccharine away however and we are left with a clear statement that we are not the deciders of what is real and what is "right" in the world. It is no wonder the writer sanitized the ending so that Job was not left in abject poverty. The horrible possibility that God can be capricious is difficult for people to accept.

Jesus told a parable about a man who hired men at dawn, noon, and sunset to work in his garden. He paid them all the same, and the men who had worked all day complained. The response was, "Don't I have the right to do what I want to with my own?" This question is at the heart of Job. If God causes a young child to be sick, is that child not His, and can He not do what He wants with what is His?

The unrelenting difficulty with understanding our place in the universe, when such a question is asked, is that there is no "security" in this world. God made us. We are His. Yet, that He would cause us harm is a real problem for us to accept. Four possibilities and twenty prophets (Psalms through Malachi) attempt to find a solution to this dilemma from the human point of view. All fail.

The gospels are the good news that we can overcome this dilemma.

## Job's Tale

The superficial story of Job is that a man with everything was tortured for no good reason by an agent of God's. The man did not deny God, but in the process tried to define and understand Him. God did not waste time on those who preached their different interpretations of God, but castigated Job for assuming that man could define Him. For the sake of the reader, God relented at the end, and restored Job to his former place, but in the process left us with the unsettling and difficult position that God could and would do with us what He wanted.

## The Philosophical Discussion

The more difficult element of the story is that no definition of God will work. Eliphaz, Bildad, and Zophar came to visit Job in his trials. Eliphaz preached that God is all powerful, that even the angels did not live up to His expectations, so Job should accept his sins, correct his actions, and change to be more in keeping with what God wanted, so that God would quit punishing him. Job rebutted him.

Bildad said that God would reward people according to their righteousness or wickedness. God was a just God who would not reward good with evil, so Job must have done something wrong. Job countered this by showing that this trial was in no way commensurate with his living.

Zophar claims that the disasters Job faced were the result of sin. This is a rather questionable point of view. No manager would pay someone for not doing what he shouldn't do, but only for what he does that is useful. Yet people have had this idea throughout history.

Eliphaz then says that Job cannot be truthful, since God deals with him in this way. Job responds. Then Bildad says that Job must be wicked, and Job responds. Zophar then claims that evil will be destroyed, and Job responds. This second round of talks again gets nowhere.

Eliphaz then questions whether man can do anything for God. Bildad claims that God is all powerful. Zophar claims that the wicked are going to be destroyed, and the third round of talk is done. At this point the three friends give up.

But Elihu has been listening in. He felt that all of the discussion was placing God in the wrong, and suggested that Job was trying to place himself in a position of being right. He suggests that Job's suffering is for Job's benefit.

## God's Answer

All changes now. It is God Himself who speaks. He shows Job that Job is not competent to even comment on what God has done. After five chapters, Job replies, "I know You are all-powerful; what you conceive, You perform. I was the man who misrepresented Your intentions with my ignorant words. You have told me about great works that I cannot understand, about marvels which are beyond me, that I cannot understand. . . . Before I knew You by hearsay but now, having seen You with my own eyes, I retract what I have said and repent in dust and ashes."

## The Meaning of Job

There is a saying that there are only two rules in getting along in a company. One is, "The boss is always right." The other is, "When the boss is wrong refer to rule one." This is essentially the meaning of Job, but the idea that you have no influence to control or change God is very depressing. If we are to be able to accept this, we must have some method that allows us to adjust to what God wants. The remainder of the Bible is devoted to investigating how we can live with God's ability to ignore us.

The controlling questions of the Bible are, "What right do you have to call anything God does fair, right, wrong, evil, or good?," "What right do you have to comment on anything that God has done, or left undone?," and "When does God allow you to comment on how He deals with anyone other than yourself?"

From Psalms through the prophets, man's possible solutions are explored. It is only when Jesus comes as God Himself in human form suffers more than we possibly will ever suffer that there is a possible answer to these questions.

# Human Attempts to Solve the Problem

The problem of how to deal with a God who created you but doesn't need you, who has created order, but has not told you what that order is, and has given you the ability to decide what should be right or wrong, but denies you the right to make that decision is a real one. How do we deal with God?

Humans tried many times and twenty-four of those possible solutions are books in the Bible. That list includes philosophies and aids (Psalms, Proverbs, Ecclesiastes, Song of Solomon, and Lamentations) and Prophets (Isaiah, Jeremiah, Ezekiel, Daniel, Hosea, Joel, Amos, Obadiah, Jonah, Micah, Nahum, Habakkuk, Zephaniah, Haggai, Zachariah, and Malachi). Because these are human solutions to a divine problem, other solutions are included by different people without any reduction to the meaning of the section. All have a point of view that man can take toward God and man's relationship with Him. All are of necessity incomplete, but most have given us a valid point of view that is helpful. The call for destruction of enemies, found in several of the prophets is a selfish wish, but most of the other points of view are enlightening.

The human response to God's power and apparent disinterest is insecurity; we fear what we do not understand. Many cultures have attempted to mollify their deity by sacrifice. Several times, on the other hand, the Bible makes it clear that God prefers justice rather than sacrifice, and that He hates such attempts to keep Him happy. Sacrificers tend to treat God as less than He is, and this attempt to limit God produces nothing but frustration. Man cannot influence, understand, or control what God is.

This fear and insecurity is evident in all the books that try to apply a human solution to dealing with God. Unless the effort to come to terms with an all powerful being comes from that being, we are always at the disadvantage of attempting something from a position of weakness. When we accept that weakness, as Job did, we realize that anything can happen to us for no reason, and the thought makes us afraid.

Fear is a great motivator. We fear terrorists, and worry about being the victims of terror. Because of this fear we support those who emphasize the fear and fail to observe that terror has been a constant element in human life since man was made. There is always someone who feels that God, who created the world and all that is in it, will reward him for destroying part of it, yet we feel that we have to spend our time and money on attempting to eliminate what will return as soon as we turn our backs.

The 9/11 attacks showed the world how such attacks should be dealt with. Men and women who accepted the responsibility for being ready to deal with such disasters gave their lives to evacuate the World Trade Center. The result was that of the thousands whose lives were at risk most did not die. This preparedness is a method of accepting the fact that terror will always be with us. Whether that terror is the result of direct human action, faulty design, earthquakes, fire, flood, or storm, it will exist whether we do anything about stopping it or not.

Fear causes us to attempt to restrict the world to our comprehension and feel that we are both able to deal with it, and should act to stop what we fear. We can choose that fear. Whether we try to stop seal hunting in the far north, or abortion, we have chosen to be arrogant enough to think that we have an answer to that fear, and that people should accept our answer as "right."

## The Ideas of the Attempts

The ideas of those who try to deal with God from a human point of view range across many feelings. We can disassociate ourselves from God, as in the Song of Songs; be cynical as in Ecclesiastes; say that all will be well in the end as in Isaiah, parts of the psalms, and parts of Ezekiel; or say that we are being punished so that we may be led to a better life as in Hosea, Micah, Haggai, Joel, and parts of Ezekiel and Daniel. We can be sad as in Lamentations; or angry, as in Jeremiah, Nahum, Amos, Zephaniah, Habakkuk, Obadiah, or parts of Ezekiel. We can try to be wise as in Proverbs; or mystical as in Daniel, Zechariah, or parts of Ezekiel. Men have had many ways of trying to get along with God. Our fears have led us to attempt to find solutions to what is God's right to deal with as he chooses.

## The Value of Human Attempts

They say that people are more fun than anybody. Human beings understand other human beings better than any other animal, and so it is clear that what humans attempt to understand covers many of the difficulties that arise because we are incapable of understanding God, but must work within His world. Each of these attempts to deal with the problem posed by the book of Job is valid within the understanding of many humans.

Ezekiel's clear statement that we are responsible for all of our actions ourselves makes it clear that we are not able to blame others for our mistakes. Jeremiah's obvious unhappiness with his angry personality shows us the need to avoid anger. Jonah's clear statement that God cares for even the cattle of the people of Nineveh shows us that we are not the only things that God cares for. Each of these lessons is valid in its own right, but is only a part of the solution to the problem.

Since only God knows enough to provide a solution, we must wait for Him to tell us how we can work with Him. The Gospels are that solution.

# The Gospels
# God's Solution to the Problem

Into this fear-filled world, God came. He didn't come as a great, all-powerful ruler, but, under Jewish law, as an illegitimate child. Joseph decided to divorce Mary informally to spare her disgrace. Only the appearance of an angel with assurances stopped this. He was homeless, with no place to lay His head. After making His statement about how people should behave, the powers that would lose so much by His example had Him crucified to protect their business interests. This crucifixion is the worst death imaginable. There is nothing that can occur to man, that God didn't suffer more.

There is a rule in management that says that a good manager will be willing to do anything that he asks his employees to do. In this case, God has shown that He is a good manager. The resurrection shows that he is God, but His life shows us how we can live. There can be no fear if what we have to do and suffer can be no more than what God has done and suffered.

This change from a fearful God to a managing God, gives us a different attitude toward the problem of how to get along with God. If God is managing the world, we can be sure that what he wants done will be accomplished. Joseph's statement in Genesis, "The evil that you planned to do me has by God's design been turned to good," and Paul's later statement, "All things work together for good to those who love God," now take on a different meaning.  God is in charge and managing the world.  We will never be asked to do more than what God himself was willing to do.  We will never be asked to suffer more than God has been willing to suffer.

There is a basic difference between the attitude that God is a fearful god who punishes, and that He is a God who manages everything.  One attitude looks to avoid hurt and punishment, and the other looks forward to actively participating in God's creation.  When a fearful servant sees an opportunity, he questions it, and asks, "Is this right?"  Usually there are enough problems to make him willing to pass up the opportunity.  A participant takes the chance, and if he fails, chalks it up to experience, learns what he can from it, and goes on.

## The Four Gospels

Each of the four Gospels has a distinct point of view toward the story of Christ.  Matthew looks to the past and reconciles the lessons of the past to the different point of view of Christ.  Mark is a simple and clear statement of what happened, with an important message that we are not expected to be winners and strong men in our own right.  Luke shows how we can look forward to understand how we can work with God.  John explains the nature of what Christ is, and how we can relate to both Him and the world we live in.

# Matthew

Matthew's role is to look back and define the difference between an attitude of fear and an attitude of participation. This is best illustrated in the parable of the talents. Talents were a unit of money in those days, and three servants were given the opportunity to participate in the monetary affairs of the master. Two took the money and ran with the challenge. The third allowed fear to keep him from participating, even to the extent of not loaning the money at interest. He is the one who was condemned. Church doctrine has tended to define usury as a sin, historically because of eventual accumulation of wealth in a few hands. That accumulation stultifies business, but the correction of that problem is to deal with the difficulty, not deny the use of usury.

The fearful person worries about many things and this worry is a sign of fear. Matthew includes a passage that tells us not to attempt to do for ourselves what God can provide. "Consider the lilies of the field. They toil not neither do they spin, yet Solomon in all his glory was not arrayed like one of these." Later, we find that God gives us someone who will tell us what to do. Allowing consideration of other philosophies and limitations limits our ability to accomplish these instructions. At a certain church event a participant had difficulty with the program. Another participant listened to her and, from his own experience, helped her to understand what was going on. The leaders of the event took him to task for acting without their authority. The church leader's requiring that his authority be in control limited what the Holy Spirit could do. A participating Christian is not bound by any authority that causes him to avoid what is of real benefit to others or himself.

The parable of the talents is part of a chapter that climaxes the book of Matthew. In it are three vital statements about how we can live a life that participates. The parable of the wedding guests tells us to be prepared at all times and not to rely on prophecies. The parable of the talents tells us to act without fear, and the discussion of the last judgment tells us what God wants us to do.

We do not know what will happen to us. Augustine once suggested that if we knew what glory we would see we would relax and wait for it, while if we knew what misery we would see, we would commit suicide. Many people live in the future or in the past, because they do not care for the present. Unfortunately, the present is all we have. If a wealthy man becomes poor, he must quickly learn a new way of life if he is to survive. By accepting what the situation is now and adjusting to it, we take the burden of caring for ourselves on our own shoulders, and give God a break.

Living without fear entails accepting whatever comes, without expecting it to always be in our favor. Subconsciously we know that 150 years from now we will not be on the earth, and whether we die at the hands of a terrorist, or in our bed at age 105, the result will be the same. Accepting our death allows us to live. We do not attempt to fend off the grim reaper, and our efforts are not hampered by attempting to stay alive. We know that death exists, but we also know that God is greater than death. Weight gain, medical mistakes, auto and plane crashes, or any other threats to us become acceptable as well. That we do not fear the risks, knowing that they exist, means that we can take the risks and move forward.

The last judgment is a discussion of what God expects of us. He did not reward anyone because of his prestige or righteousness, but only for their contribution to others. One mistake that many make is to say that this contribution should be made without pay, but Christ also made it clear that "a laborer is worthy of his hire." So what God is asking is for the supermarket bagboy to feed the hungry, the textile factory worker to clothe the naked, and so on. Whatever we do for others, whether paid or not, is our gift to God.

Matthew emphasizes the rules that men should follow: don't judge, pray in secret, don't worship earthly treasures, keep holy things holy, and so on. He also states that laws will not change. "Do not kill" still applies because this law is self-enforcing. But just avoiding what is wrong is not enough. A manager pays his help for what they accomplish for him, not for what they do not do that is wrong. A managing God does not reward us for avoiding sin, but for what we do for Him and for others.

Not everyone has the same job in any well-managed company. When Jesus is asked if people should pay taxes, He doesn't just answer that question. His response is, "Render unto Caesar the things that are Caesar's, and unto God the things that are God's." Things that are Caesar's not only include taxes, but when needed, votes, obedience, and information as to the realities that underlie changes in the laws. Things that are God's include tithes, but also include prayers and active support of neighbors as described in the parable of the Good Samaritan.

Here also is the explanation of the separation of church and state. It is clear that the purpose of any government is to assure that people can work together. To do this, basic laws must be enforced without forgiveness. If a law is not enforced it is not a law. But the Christian is not dealing with the basic laws. He is asked to do far more "Be ye perfect, even as the Father in heaven is perfect." This is obviously impossible, so it follows that we should forgive even "until seventy times seven."

In a similar manner, every person has his own task and his own purpose, assigned by God through the Holy Spirit. That assignment may be specific, as was the assignment of Joan of Arc or Bernadette of Lourdes, but the Holy Spirit is not limited to people with specific assignments. A child who is avidly interested in being a mechanic, spends his time around cars, and become expert at the care of automobiles is as surely called to his task as any other person. The example of Abraham, as described in the earlier chapter about Genesis, illustrates that the call may not even be ascribed to God, but simply happens. With an all-powerful and managing God, whatever we do, whether evil or good, will be used to accomplish His purpose.

Matthew looks at Christ in the context of the world around us, and gives us confidence that we can live here in peace.

# Mark

Matthew is a story of what we should do. Ideas of propriety and the law are significant in that book. Mark differs. It deals with people, people just like us, who fail to understand, and yet are chosen by Christ to do what he wants done. Mark is shorter as well. It gives the whole story in digest form. Here the writer does not look back to the past, as Matthew does, or forward to the future as Luke does, but simply tells the story of how people interacted with Jesus. Some of these interactions were miracles of healing.

Some people question these miracles. Could they have happened as they are written? Accepting our inability to understand that we aren't able to verify an event makes us somewhat uneasy, but it is more in tune with reality than trying to prove a negative. The effort to deny that the miracles happened is fruitless. There is an old saying, "If you are asked to bet that there is no flea that can throw an elephant out the window, do not accept the bet, for you will soon meet that flea and that elephant." Proving a negative is impossible.

Such an effort also denies the power of God. If God created order and science is the study of order, it is important to remember that God is not bound by His creation. Miracles can occur at any time, but they are God's miracles, not ours.

Mark makes it clear that God works with men as they are. One example is the "Jews" who crucified Jesus.

# Luke

Luke looks forward. The best example of the emphasis of Luke is the parable of the Prodigal Son. But the statements that are overlooked in that story are as important as the ones that are not. The Prodigal spends his inheritance. At the end, it is made clear that he will not share in anything else from his father. The story is not about restoration to the conditions that applied earlier. When the Prodigal thinks about being a servant in his father's house, there is no indication that that is not what occurs.

Another key phase is, "He came to himself." By recognizing the situation as it was, he was able to let go of those things that held him back. We all hold on to baggage that restricts our ability to move forward. A certain minister was receiving a salary of $10,000 from his church when the average salary of a minister was only $6,000. (This was many years

# The Gospels, God's Solution to the Problem

ago.) He could not be expected to hear a call to move to another church, because he would have to accept a cut in pay. His usefulness to that church was gone, but God couldn't make him listen because he could not hear over the sound of his income.

The Prodigal acted on his understanding. He returned to his father and asked to be accepted as a servant. The rejoicing of the father tends to lead us to expect the Prodigal's reinstatement as a son, but that does not follow, when the father clearly states to the other son that "All that I have will be yours." The understanding that we act on our understanding of reality, and move forward from where we are is the essence of Luke.

Some years ago, a younger daughter left home, and spent her life in Washington, D. C. When she was old, she returned to her home, and expected that her father would have given her something in his will. She refused to accept that the stay-at-home sister had received all the inheritance, and spent her remaining years and resources trying to change that will. Had she recognized that the reality was not in her favor and used what remained of her resources to go forward from where she was, her last years would not have been spent in poverty and penury.

Luke asks us to accept life as it is and move forward, leaving our unnecessary baggage behind.

# John

Matthew ties Jesus to the past. Mark ties Jesus to people. Luke asks us to allow Jesus to guide us in the future. John tells us who Jesus was and what Jesus wants. There is no chronological correspondence between John and the other Gospels. Matthew, Mark, and Luke tell us that Jesus cleansed the temple just before his arrest. John starts the story there, only placing the philosophical basis for the story, John the Baptist's ministry, and the miracle of the wedding at Cana earlier. (The wedding at Cana shows that Jesus was not averse to celebration.) The cleansing of the temple shows that Jesus condemned the system as it was. This system of sacrifices and monetary worship harks back to the time of Ezra, and the moneychangers can be said to be Ezraites.

In our discussion of Ezra we noted that Christ condemned most of what Ezra and Nehemiah did. Ezra had the impure wives divorced. Christ condemned divorce. John, after describing a conversation with Nicodemus and the endorsement of John the Baptist, tells us, in a conversation with a Samaritan woman, that people will no longer worship in a set place, but in spirit and in truth. Ezra and Nehemiah demanded worship in the temple in Jerusalem, and even had people move to Jerusalem to accomplish this. This contrast illustrates that Christ condemned the actions of those who followed Ezra. Other examples of this condemnation include Christ's statements on purity and sin.

John spells out for us the purpose and identity of Christ.

# The Concluding Section

Once we have spelled out the problem in the Bible, and God's reasonable resolution, we need to wrap up the story. And the last part of the Bible does just that. While the Disciples feel that they need to replace one of their own by lot, God chooses to do it in His own way. Paul's job is to clarify the meaning of the gospels. His life story and the activities of the other disciples after Christ's ascension are the subject of Acts. Romans spells out the understanding that laws that are needed when people do not love one another are immaterial when people do. It also makes it clear that what we do to satisfy God is wasted effort. By doing what God wants because of our love for Him, we are doing what God created us to do.

First Corinthians helps us understand how we can get along together in love. A discussion of sex makes it clear that Paul is offering his opinion, but also makes it clear that the baggage of our sexual nature should be cared for. He also points out our responsibility for each other in not leading each other astray, our need not to acquire more unnecessary baggage by dealing with idols.

Then come three chapters on subjects that are vital: respect for God, respect for and acceptance of each other, and the nature of love.

Paul is sometimes difficult to follow. Such a situation allows interpretations of his teachings by emphasizing what is in favor of the person doing the interpretation. Such a case occurs in Ephesians where Paul admonishes women be subject to their husband in two sentences, and then spends three sentences admonishing men to behave in such a manner that women will be willing to be subject. When we emphasize the women's instruction without mentioning the men's, we find ourselves in real difficulties.

The remaining letters of Paul deal with specific situations that arise from our choosing to be part of God's creation, instead of choosing to be proud of ourselves.

Hebrews tells us that the ritual laws spelled out in the Old Testament no longer apply. Some other letters admonish us to be strong in the faith, and the Revelation of John starts by continuing this admonition

Then John goes off on a different tack. Essentially the dream that he reveals tells us that God is worthy of all praise, and we are part of that glorious future. This is a grand way to conclude a story that is a whole, entire, and complete book — the Bible.

We often refer to the Bible as an authority. When we limit our understanding of God to what is in the book, we fail to understand why the

Bible was written. The Holy Spirit is not limited to what is written. He has the power to give us God's instruction whenever and wherever he chooses, but without the Bible, we might not recognize some special role that God may have chosen for us.

The Bible is a whole book and introduces us to God.

# Summary

God did write a consistent narrative. There are five points that come from that knowledge. These points are:

1. The Bible is a whole, with a consistent theme throughout.
2. The Bible is an introduction to God and His authority, and has no authority in and of itself.
3. God is the creator, owner, and manager of the universe and under the "ownership" law of management is always right. The second law of management also applies, "When the Boss is wrong, refer to rule one."
4. We are only a small part of God's creation. We are limited by our environment, and cannot decide what is right and what is wrong except within that environment, and then only to the extent that that decision is approved by God.
5. We are an important part of God's creation, given a task, no matter how small, that God has felt important enough to have created us for. As such we will be provided with what we need.

## The Bible is a whole, with a consistent theme throughout.

Because the parts of the Bible fulfill a role, the use of any part outside the context of its role changes their meaning, and destroys the idea that makes it important. The story of the minister who preached against the "Top Knot" hairdo because the Bible said, "Top Knot come down," is an extreme example. (The text quoted read, "let him who is upon the housetop not come down.) We choose to use less obvious examples often. The "sin" of Onan is used to condemn a certain sex act, when the role of that statement is to describe what happens when people fail to take responsibility for fulfilling their role in the community.

The most flagrant examples of this attempt to manipulate the Bible are where certain sections are used for the purpose self enrichment. The men who crucified Jesus did not do so for the good of the people, but to continue to receive the benefits of their jobs in the temple. To be labeled "A den of thieves" is not conducive to continuing to receive profits from the temple environment.

It is not easy to accept the role that God gives you when that role involves pain and difficulties. Luckily, most of the roles involved do not, and we grow complacent in our prosperity. Because we do, we make the mistake of using our evaluation of the situation and not God's. When that happens, we are tempted, as Job's wife tempted Job, to "Curse God and die." It is not easy to respond as Job did.

# The Bible Is an Introduction to God and His Authority, and Has No Authority In and Of Itself

When Jesus said, "What God has joined together, let not man put asunder," we must not assume that He also meant "What man has joined together, let not God put asunder." We as humans make mistakes. When those mistakes occur, God does not usually interfere. But if God's plan requires that they be rectified, the words that He uses in the Bible do not limit Him. God is the authority, and exercises that authority through the Holy Spirit, not by a rigid adherence to a set rule.

To have faith that the Holy Spirit can and does act in our lives is a difficult concept when he can use any incident he chooses, and directs our lives in such seemingly insignificant ways. It is easier to make the Bible our idol, and limit ourselves to safe and familiar paths by ignoring the opportunities that come to us when we are open to the direction of the Holy Spirit.

Thus we make the Bible the authority, and leave God out of the mix. Our lives become stale and limited, but we feel safe in them. The censoring of the book OF MICE AND MEN by a so called Christian school deprived those students of the knowledge of what true love can be in difficult situations. In the book that true love involved the deliberate murder of a man's brother. It is difficult to understand that love could demand this in any normal situation. The book required the reader to look closely at what true love means. However, the students were safe from an "immoral" book.

God is in charge in any situation, and is not limited by our interpretation of the Bible.

## God Is the Creator, Owner, and Manager of the Universe.

God is the creator, owner, and manager of the universe and under the ownership law of management is always right. The second law of management also applies, "When the Boss is wrong, refer to rule one."

We are often tempted to ask, "Why would God allow a little child to suffer?" Were it not true that God, through Christ, has suffered more than will be possible for anyone to suffer, we could feel cheated when such things happen. But it is God's world and we are His creation in it. It is not our world to decide how things will happen, and it takes an understanding faith to allow God to be God, rather than demand that He fit our conception of Him.

## We Are Only a Small Part of God's Creation.

We are limited by our environment, and cannot decide what is right and what is wrong except within that environment, and then only to the extent that that decision is approved by God. Moreover, our belief that we are "Little lower than the angels" gives us the false impression that we are more important than other creations that God has made. With that in mind we try to maintain that importance by setting standards that do not fit our lives as God created us. We chose to deny that we have failed to live up to these standards and fail to allow God to forgive us because we cannot forgive ourselves. We agonize over what has happened in the past, and can never be changed. To live in the past by allowing ourselves to feel guilty about something that can not be changed is to deny ourselves the freedom to look toward the future.

It is also a type of arrogance to believe that God, who has created the universe, the world, billions of people, and even more animals of other types, has to be concerned with anyone's penny-ante sins. Perhaps that is why He stated that all sins are going to be forgiven except refusing to work with the Holy Spirit. To accept this forgiveness is galling to many people's egos. It is easier to dwell on them than to get on with living. It takes an understanding that we are not as important as we would like to be.

## We Are an Important Part of God's Creation.

But while we are not as important as we would like to think, we are an important part of God's creation. We are given a task, no matter how small, that God has felt important enough to have created you for. As such you will be provided with what you need.

The Psalms say, "Cast thy burden upon the Lord, and he shall sustain thee.'" When you worry, when life is too much for you, when you face frustrations or challenges, these words should echo in your mind. Each of us faces every one of these problems.

We find life hard. Often we make it harder by thinking that we should be like others whom we admire, and whose life appears to be easier than ours. Appearances in others can be different from reality. We only see what is visible from our point of view, and what people are willing to let others see, brief snapshots of behavior that is comfortable for them. We hear others talk of their perfect children, their well-paying and interesting careers, their adventurous lives lacking boredom. Our life--in all its aspects--is seldom like anyone else's life. Parts of life may be marvelous. We should be happy for them. But let's keep things in perspective. Heartache, pain, or discontent happens to everyone at some time. If you could see into anyone's heart, you will find some cause for sadness.

But our lives are not all sadness. Anguish and peace come together. Hope of happiness comes with despair. Life is both the good *and* the bad, celebration *and* hurt, enjoyment *and* difficulties. If we realize this, we will understand and feel less threatened when all is not as we would wish it to be.

Life is not a race. The success of others does not discourage those who find real joy. Making the best of their own situations interests them more. Each life has its own purpose. We are not competing against anyone else in our families, our careers or in life. Each person has been given abilities to fulfill the purposes God has given them. Let go of the idea that someone else is your example and do the best you can each day to smile, to be kind, to love, and to face each new day with joy. The Psalmist tells us that the Lord neither slumbers nor sleeps. He will provide our needs.